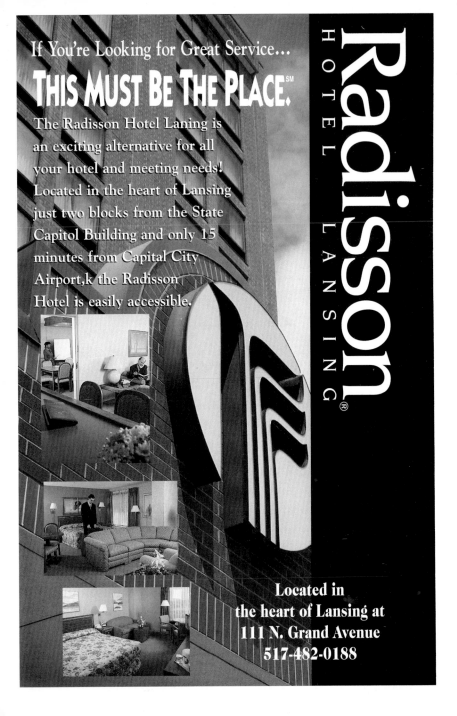

The Lansing Regional Chamber of Commerce:
A Part of Lansing *Through the Years*

In 1901, a few dozen local businessmen formed a group, known as the Lansing Businessman's Association, for the purpose of recruiting a young auto manufacture to Lansing. The group purchases a large parcel of land left vacant when the State Fair was moved to Detroit and offered it, free of charge and with no strings attached, to Ransom E. Olds if he would move his growing automobile company back to Lansing form Detroit. No stranger to Lansing, having opened th first Olds Motor Works in Lansing before moving the company to Detroit,l Olds agreed to build a new factory on the fairground site, after fire destroyed his Detroit plant.

In 1914, the association changed its name to the Lansing Chamber of Commerce, then to the Chamber of Commerce of Greater Lansing in 1956, and to the Lansing Regional Chamber of Commerce in 1974. Meanwhile, many key members of the Lansing business community assumed positions of leadership in the Chamber to promote cooperation among area businesses.

Today, the Chamber can claim credit for a variety of tri-county developments as it continues to represent regional interests in government, economic development, education and small business matters. the Chamber is a key player when it comes to small business assistance, and provides a number of services, including financial counseling, seminars, assistance in cutting through governmental "red tape" and other entrepreneurial support services to new and existing businesses.

Chamber of Commerce Building
- Prudden Municipal Auditorium

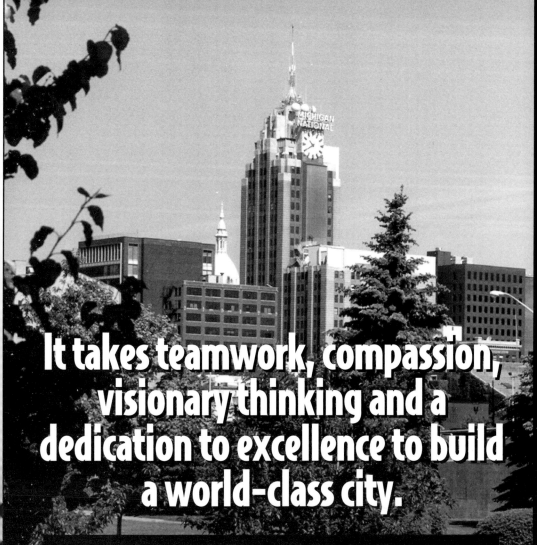

Through the Years

A Pictorial History of Greater Lansing
1847 - 1997

Published by Visions Sports Management Group, Inc.

Printed by Walsworth Printing, Marceline, MIssouri 64658
Printed in the U.S.A. • ISBN: 0-9658933-0-8

Note from the Publisher:

This historical publication will never claim to be scientific and absolute in its production or research. There are many sites we have been unable to include in this publication. This was due to the overwhelming amount of photographs reviewed. We will, however, sound the trumpets on the sole intent of its origin, capturing a handful of Greater Lansing's unique and exciting faces, places, and moments in its first 150 years. Participation through the submission of photographs from all generations of Lansing's community especially created an intimate portrait of our town. A special thanks to Ray Walsh, photo/caption consultant for his hard work at making this book a success.

Seymour A. Ayres, 1880

He went through thousands of photographs in the selection process and made many tough decisions on image usage. Also, special thanks go to a dedicated Linda Peckham, our chapter introduction author. The precious children pictured below separated by over a century truly epitomize history past and present. These photos represent more than a thousand words; more significantly they lay claim to a thousand dreams, all taking place through the years!

Vision Sports Management Group
Michael J. Ward, Camron Gnass, Ken Landau, R. Jon Harpst and Doug Cooper

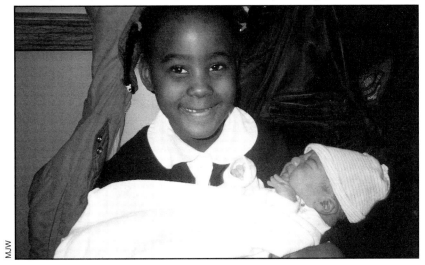

Gabrielle Marie Ward and newborn brother Langston Ellison Ward, 1994

Cover Design & Interior Layout by Camron Gnass, Vision Creative

Introduction: Your Hometown Authors

In June of 1847 when the plat was registered for the "Town of Michigan, Michigan," lots began to sell immediately. This land, where no town had ever existed, was chosen to be the new capital city of the State of Michigan.

When Michigan had become a state in 1837, a temporary capital was located in Detroit. Ten years later, many towns, especially Owosso and Marshall, sought to become the permanent capital, and most people thought that a move to the interior of the state would make the capital safer and encourage settlement.

But after heated debates, in a surprise move in March of 1847 the legislators chose a wilderness site in Lansing Township to become the new capital.

Settlers raced to develop a town. It would be created whole by those who arrived first. They saw their future. Excitement ran high.

Linda Peckham & Ray Walsh

By the end of December 1847, a capitol building had been erected and a town was growing. The Legislature was seated in January 1848. In April, the name was changed to "Lansing."

Before 1847, only a handful of settlers lived near James Seymour's dam and mill in what is now North Lansing. By 1850, the population of Lansing had jumped to 1,200 people. Now, the Greater Lansing area is home to more than 300,000 people.

From its beginning, Lansing's history has been entwined with the State of Michigan's. On its 150th birthday, Lansing is one of the oldest capital cities in the United States.

Through the Years offers a pictorial history of Lansing's 150 years of development. These photos, many from the private collections of businesses and families and never before published, provide a unique look at our city. We know you will find it as exciting as we do.

Linda R. Peckham
President, Historical Society of Greater Lansing
Executive Director, Lansing Capital Sesquicentennial

Ray Walsh
Photo/Caption Consultant

Foreword: Gov. John M. Engler & Lansing Mayor David C. Hollister

STATE OF MICHIGAN
OFFICE OF THE GOVERNOR
LANSING

JOHN ENGLER
GOVERNOR

Dear Friends:

As Governor of Michigan, it gives me great pleasure to be a part of *Through the Years: A Pictorial History of Greater Lansing 1847-1997*.

When Lansing was selected as our state's capital in 1847, it was referred to as the "wilderness capital" and literally had to be built from scratch before the legislature could convene in 1848. During the last 150 years, however, Lansing has grown tremendously. What was once a primarily lumbering and fur-trapping area is now one of the greatest manufacturing centers in the nation, on the cutting edge of new technologies and innovations.

Although the City has witnessed sweeping changes, its residents still cherish their rural, agricultural roots and have great pride in their home town. As a long-time resident of this community, I share that pride and hope that Lansing continues to prosper for many years to come.

Through the Years will bring Lansing's rich history to life, memorializing the past for future generations. It is an important addition to the City's historical record and I am certain that it will be a valued keepsake for Lansing residents and for citizens throughout our great state.

Sincerely,

John Engler
John Engler
Governor

OFFICE OF THE MAYOR
9th Floor, City Hall
124 West Michigan Avenue
Lansing, Michigan 48933-1694
(517) 483-4141 (Voice)
(517) 483-4479 (TDD)
(517) 483-6066 (FAX)

David C. Hollister, Mayor   June, 1997

It is my pleasure to introduce this commemorative book celebrating the Sesquicentennial of Lansing as the Capital City of the State of Michigan. This is the first major publication of photographs of Lansing in some years. It contains 150 years of memories and will be a collector's item of this Sesquicentennial Year.

Although it was chosen as a place in the wilderness to locate a capital city and had no distinction as a seat of politics, Lansing became and continues to be a community that cherishes its politics.

Lansing is a microcosm of American life and history. It is one of the nation's oldest automotive manufacturing centers and just last year was recognized again as the "Car Capital of North America," having produced more cars than any other city.

The Grand River, the center of early settlement, is now the center of the City's renaissance as the new stadium, convention center, river plaza and river walk, the revitalization of "Oldtown," and new housing development bring people back to the river as the center of the city.

Lansing has always been a community that reflects the diversity of American society, drawing people from all over the United States and the world. Lansing citizens come from over 100 countries and weave a beautiful tapestry of cultures here.

The Greater Lansing region is a center of education and medicine, of arts and theater, of cultivated parks and gardens as well as areas of natural beauty.

And most important, Lansing is a city of neighborhoods, where families take pride in their homes and their friendships and build their futures together.

This book captures our past and the spirit that makes Lansing the special community it has been, it is and it is continuing to become. Thanks to the families and organizations who submitted photographs, many of them never made public before. Thanks to Visions Sports who edited and published this volume. And thanks to the Lansing Capital Sesquicentennial Commission, the Historical Society of Greater Lansing and the many businesses who helped underwrite this venture.

D. C. Hollister

"Equal Opportunity Employer"

Table of Contents

All photos are noted respective to their collector or photographer. **This mark indicates an original Leavenworth Photograph.

Chapter 1

In the Beginning

Michigan, Michigan

1847 - 1897

Born as "Michigan," Michigan, but renamed "Lansing" within a year, the town soon had two mills, hotels, general stores, a school, three religious groups, three bridges over the Grand River, a financial exchange, and a newspaper.

The 1850s and '60s brought more of the same, and added the opening of Michigan Female College, Michigan Agricultural College, the House of Corrections for Boys, the Torrent Engine Company (firefighters), Oak Park Cemetery, a high school, and a plank road to Howell.

A. Clark & Co. was building carriages, Bement & Sons produced farm implements, Mead's Hall opened, and the railroads finally arrived. The Civil War cost many lives. Population in 1870: 5,200.

By 1897, the population stood at nearly 16,000. Investors had founded banks, the Gas Light Co., the City Water Works, and industries related to carriage manufacturing. They established a police department, the first kindergarten in Michigan, and many social and industrial societies.

After its first 50 years, Lansing was a thriving city, worthy of its 1847 promise.

Tintype of an unidentified pioneer family (ca. 1880's). -State of Michigan Archives

The old "pearl" or Christian Breisch Mill, a landmark in north Lansing, erected in 1848. It stood on the corner of Turner Street and East Grand River Avenue. It was torn down in 1927. -Lansing Public Library

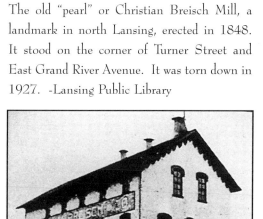

Believed to be Lansing's first frame house, built in 1847 by James M. Turner. Years later it was torn down to make room for auto body company. -Lansing Public Library

A glimpse of old Washington Avenue North, 1860.
-Lansing Public Library

Log cabin built in Meridian Township by Henry C. Ayres in 1862. Ayres built a hat hook from a limb crotch. The property this cabin built upon is now owned by Michigan State University.
-Frances M. Coryell

	1847	1850	1860
Population	88 - (Lansing Twp., 1845)	1,216 - (Lansing)	3,100
Education	1847 First School: Eliza Powell, teacher	1855 Michigan Female College opened 1857 Michigan Agricultural College opened, First land-grant college in nation	1861 First Board of Education, Lansing 1862-1885 Dr. T.C. Abbot, President, M.A.C. 1863-1902 Dr. Robert C. Kedzie, Prof. of Chem, M.A.C. 1865 First Lansing High School

1875 Lansing flood looking west across the dam at North Lansing. One of the bridges washed out by the flood is in the foreground, hung up on the dam.
-David R. Caterino

George and Orselia Pease (ca.1870's). The parents of Lansing's first white child, W. Marshall Pease, born July 4, 1845.
-Donna B. Peterson

1870	1880	1890
5,241	8,319	13,102

1870 Women Admitted to M.A.C.
1871 Michigan Female College closed
1871 First Kindergarten in Mich. (Stebbins)
1870-1910 Dr. William J. Beal, Head of Botany, M.A.C.
1875 $50,000 High School (Old Central)
1876 Farmers' Institutes, M.A.C.

1880 Michigan School for the Blind
1885 Horticultural School, first in nation, M.A.C., by Liberty Hyde Bailey

1894 "Short Courses," M.A.C.
1896 "Women's Courses," M.A.C.

National Guard (1897) mustered to go to Island Lake at opening of Spanish-American War.
-State of Michigan Archives

This photo by J.H. Scotford shows E. W. Dart in full parade dress as a member of Knight's Templar. (ca. 1878) -Rambo Collection

Another photo by J.H. Scotford with Edward W. Sparrow in Knights Templar uniform (ca. 1878). -Rambo Collection

1847	1850	1860

| Government | 1842 Lansing Township org.
1847 Lansing Township chosen as new site for state capital
1847 Town platted and named "Michigan," Michigan
1847 First Post Office (Geo. Peck, PM)
1848 First meeting of State Legislature at Lansing, Capitol dedicated
1848 Town name changed to "Lansing" | 1850 First Constitutional Convention
1851 Oak Park Cemetery est.
1856 House of Corrections, for boys
1857 Torrent Engine Company (fire) org.
1859 City of Lansing incorporated; first mayor, H.H. Smith | 1861-64 Austin Blair, Civil War Governor
1869 Harriet A Tenney named State Librarian, first woman |

Lt. Luther B. Baker and his horse Buckskin. In 1865 led the party that tracked down and captured John Wilkes Booth, the assassin of President Abraham Lincoln. Baker moved to Lansing in 1866. (Composite photo is ca. 1887). -David R. Caterino

First Larch Street School (ca. 1870), later the home of Pilgrim Congregational Church. -Lansing Public Library

A flyer passed out at the train stations advertising the Lansing House Hotel, (ca. 1870's). -M.S.U. Museum

1870	1880	1890
1873 Mt. Hope Cemetery est.	1882 Capitol of 1847 burns	1893 Lansing Police Department
1873 Mich. State Board of Health (Kedzie/Baker)	1885 City Water Works	1894 New Post Office at Michigan & Capitol
1879 New State Capitol dedicated Elijah E. Myers, Architect		1896 New City Hall at Ottawa & Capitol

Franklin Avenue (now Grand River Ave.) wooden bridge, erected in 1867 over the Grand River. This bridge was swept away April 1, 1875 during the spring flood.
-Lansing Public Library

Donna Savage, age 9, and Grove Keith, age 5, enjoying a magazine; August 1897.
-David R. Caterino

Waverly Park steamboat (ca. 1880's).
-State of Michigan Archives

	1847	1850	1860
Societies Clubs & The Arts		1853 First Masonic Lodge 1854 Ingham County Agricultural Society and annual fair	1866 Central Michigan Ag Society 1865 Mead's Hall 1868 Lansing Liederkranz Club
Religious Groups	1846 First Methodist 1847 First Presbyterian 1849 St. Paul's Episcopal	1851 First Baptist 1852 Universalist 1855 First Lutheran (Emanuel) 1856 St. Mary Catholic	1864 German Methodist Episcopalians 1864 Congregationalists 1866 African Methodist Episcopalians (Trinity AME)

Construction workers take a break to pose for a picture. Note the hard working man in the pipe protruding from the wall (ca. 1880's).
-State of Michigan Archives

1870

1871 Lansing Library & Literary Association
1872 Ingham Co. Historical & Pioneer Society
1872 Grand River Boat Club
1873 Buck's Opera House
1873 Pioneer Society of Mich.
1874 Lansing Woman's Club
1877 YMCA

1880

1889 YWCA

1886 St. Paul's German Evangelical

1890

1894 Matinee Musicale (Kate Kedzie)
1895 Women's Historical Society
1896 Woman's Hospital Association
       (became Sparrow Hospital 1912)
1896 DAR, Lansing Chapter
1898 Statue of Gov. Blair dedicated
       (Front Walk of Capitol)

1890 Central Methodist Church, Ottawa St.
1892 First Baptist Church, Capitol Ave,
       Bowd & Mead, Architects

Charles L. Sattler's Grocery, Crockery & Glassware store at 220 E. Grand River Avenue (ca. 1880's). -David R. Caterino

Rear view of 220 E. Grand River (ca. 1880's). The Sattler family lived above the store. This was their remarkable backyard. -David R. Caterino

	1847	1850	1860

Business & Industry		
1847 Bush & Thomas, Store, Main St.	1850 First Financial Exchange, J.C. Bailey	1864 Second National Bank of Lansing (First Nat'l. never opened)
1847 C.C. Darling, Store & Bakery		1866 A. Clark & Co. (Carriages)
1847 James Turner, Merchant, N. Lansing	1855 Lansing Republican, weekly news	1868 Kositchek's (Men's Clothing)
1845 Sawmill, N. Lansing (Page/Seymour)	1855 Pearl Mills (Mosley)	1869 Bement & Sons, Foundry (Peerless Plow)
1847 Seymour Hotel N. Lansing	1857 Oriental Mills (Reitz and Thoman)	
1848 Gristmill, N. Lansing (Hart, Danforth, HH Smith)	1858 James I. Mead, Tannery	
1848 Buck's Furniture, Wash. & Ionia		
1848 The Free Press, newspaper of "Michigan," Michigan		

Octagon house built 1854 by Col. Whitney at the corner of Washington Avenue and Kalamazoo Street. The cupola on top was called a belvedere.
-State of Michigan Archives

Robert Barker, 1860's, manufactured brick and tile in North Lansing from 1871-88, was steward and bookkeeper for the Michigan School For the Blind, then became Superintendent in 1859.
-David R. Caterino

1870

1870 Mineral Well Hotel
1872 Lansing Iron Works
1872 Lansing Gas Light Co. (E. F. Cooley)
1872 Flour Mill (J.I. Mead)
1872 Lansing National Bank
1872 Michigan Supply Co
(Plumbing & Steam Fittings)
1873 Lansing Journal
1873 Lansing Improvement Co.
1875 Central Michigan Savings Bank

1880

1880 P.F. Olds (Steam Engines)
1880 James Henry Moores: Logging Camps
1880 Telephone Exchange
1881 Michigan Millers Mutual Insurance Co.
1881 Lansing Wheelbarrow Works
1883 Rollin H. Person, Law Firm
(Fraser Trebilcock Davis & Foster)
1885 Lansing Wheel Co. (W.K. Prudden)
1886 Friedland (scrap)
1886 City National Bank
1886 Union Savings & Loan
1889 Furniture Factory, James W. Potter

1890

1890 Capitol Savings & Loan (Community First)
1891 A.M. Cummins, Law Firm
(Cummins Woods & Panek)
1891 Silver Lead Paint (O'Leary)
1892 Lansing State Svgs Bank (First of America)
1893 Financial Panic
1895 Young Bros. & Daley
1896 Bates Engine Co. (Wohlert Corp.)
1896 Patent on Gas (vapor) Engine, R.E. Olds
1897 Patent on Motor Carriage, R.E. Olds
1897 Olds Motor Vehicle Co.

Marriage certificate of Chester B. Leonard and Emma Parker. Married at the Free Will Baptist Church, September 14, 1881.
-David R. Caterino

1880's "rush hour" in downtown Lansing.
- Lansing Public Library

1847	1850	1860
Transportation		
1847 First bridge, at Main St.	1858 Plank Road, Lansing to Howell	1861 Amboy, Lansing, Traverse Bay RR
1847 Second bridge, at Franklin St.	(Seymour, Turner, Smith)	1866 Jackson, Lansing, Saginaw RR
(Grand River Ave. N. Lansing)		(Merged into Mich. Central 1916)
1848 Bridge at Michigan Ave.		1869 Ionia & Lansing RR (CSX 1987)
Events		
1843 First dam, N. Lansing (John Burchard)	1857 First major fire	1865 Luther B. Baker captures John Wilkes Booth
1844 Burchard drowns; dam abandoned	1858 Chief Okemos dies, age unknown	
1844 Pages and Rolfes rebuild dam		
1845 First Fourth of July Celebration		

Lake Shore and Michigan Southern Railroad Depot in 1888.
-Lansing Illustrated

Franklin Avenue (later E. Grand River Avenue) in North Lansing in 1888.
-Lansing Illustrated

Lansing Fuel Company in 1888.
-Lansing Illustrated

1870	1880	1890

1810 Peninsular Ry RR (GTW Ry 1900)
1873 Lake Shore & Mich Southern
      (Merged into NY Central 1915)

1886 Steam engine vehicle, R. E. Olds

1890 Electric Street Car
1896 Gasoline (vapor) automobile,
      R.E. Olds (Frank Clark, carriage)

1871 Mark Twain at Mead's Hall
1875 The Great Ice Jam & Flood
      (5 of 6 bridges destroyed)
1877 O.M. Barnes' House

1888 Seven Financial Conspiracies,
      by Sarah Emery

Bailey Buck, R.G. Edmonds, Walter Bailey, Hart Row, J.P. Edmonds, Frank Hertzler, R.G. Jones; all Lansing residents (ca. 1888).
-Lansing Public Library

Civil War veteran Colonel Frederick Schneider and family in front of their gazebo, August 28, 1889. The gazebo still stands behind the Schneider home at 726 Seymour Street.
-David R. Caterino

An old monarch of the Lansing landscape was the standpipe in the 100 block of South Cedar Street, erected in 1885 by the Board of Water and Light commissioners, and dismantled in August 1949.
-Lansing Public Library

The "Barnes Castle" built in 1877 on Capitol Avenue and East Main Street. Major Orlando Mack Barnes entertained many State Supreme Court Justices, state officials, and significant business people. Barnes made his fortune in timber and railroads.
-State of Michigan Archives

Grand Avenue in 1890. Bement
Foundry began operations in 1870,
producing numerous bobsleds and
eventually supplying the automotive
industry.
-Lansing Public Library

John F. Rouse mourning photo,
died April 1, 1891.
-David R. Caterino

Grand River Boat
Club, 1898, club
room (second floor).
-Lansing Public
Library

Bement baseball team
(ca. 1890's).
-Lansing Public Library

Mae McKibbin (ca. 1890)
She later taught and
became principal at the
Townsend Street School.
-Donna B. Peterson

First Baptist Church, built in 1892
on corner of Capitol Avenue. Note
the romanesque revival architecture.
-State of Michigan Archives

Out in backyard playing with mom, dad looking on (ca. 1890's). -Lansing Public Library

Jim Newcomer's Second Hand Shop (ca. 1893).
-State of Michigan Archives

Photo by Cheney and Christmas of early Lansing business-men. In the back row Rob Jones, Walter Bailey, Jim Edmonds, and Frank Row. In the front Bailey Buck and Rob Edmonds are among those present (ca. late 1890's).
-Rambo Collection

Otto Ziegler's family on a picnic (ca. 1897), Otto Ziegler is on the left.
-David R. Caterino

Lansing Bicycle Club gathers in front of the State Capitol (ca. 1880's).
-State of Michigan Archives

Schultz Barrel Factory (ca. 1890). -State of Michigan Archives

Lansing Steam and
Die Works (ca. 1890's).
-State of Michigan Archives

Turner Grocery
Company , 100 East
Michigan Avenue
(ca. 1895), notice
Dr. F.A. Jones on
second floor.
-Lansing Public
Library

Interior of butcher shop (ca. 1890's). -State of Michigan Archives

Storefront of butcher shop with meats hanging, ready for sale (ca. 1890's). -State of Michigan Archives

J.H. Larrabee Bicycles and Guns storefront (ca. 1890). -Lansing Public Library

Lansing's first fire department in 1895. Station number 1 was located at 112 East Allegan Street. The firewagon on the far left was used as a chemical wagon to mix water and soda solution to help extinguish fires. City Hall is on the floor above. -Lansing Public Library

Florence Danielson, Cassie Gates, Ethel Sheets, Lucy Safford, Donna Savage, Grace Morgan, Grove Keith, unidentified (not in order); October 1897. -David R. Caterino

Chapter 2

Turning the Page
The Wheels Are Rolling
1897 - 1940

When Ransom E. Olds drove a horseless carriage away from his father's engine shop on River Street one night in 1886, he was referred to as "that darned Olds kid." But in 1897, after receiving patents on his gas vapor engine and motor carriage, Olds organized the Olds Motor Vehicle Co., and Lansing came to the attention of the world.

Many Lansing companies began to supply the automotive industry. Such companies as Clark Carriage, Prudden Wheel, and Bates Engine, forerunner of Wohlert Corp., gained wide notice.

Olds, creator of the Curved Dash Runabout, left his namesake company in 1904 and established the REO car and REO truck companies, soon world-renowned. In 1908, the Oldsmobile nameplate became part of the new General Motors.

Partly because of the diversity of its automotive industry, Lansing enjoyed a stable economic base for many years.

David R. Caterino

In the late 1890's R.E. Olds pulls out of his garage. With him are his wife Metta and their two daughters.
-Rambo Collection

Chester B. Leonard's Cottage Grocery at 333-335 S. Butler Avenue (ca. 1900), left to right: John Graham, C. B. Leonard, Orla Bailey, Harry Flint, Horse Fly, Fred Weaver, Mac Alies. -David R. Caterino

Gladys Maltby, Junior Brooks, May Mc Carthy, Lulu Bacon, Lucile Titus, Glen Harris, Otto Scheiber, Grove Keith (not in order); third grade, Townsend Street School, December 1899. -David R. Caterino

Interior of H. Merton Clark Jewelry and Paint Store, Washington Avenue, 1900.

Laying the cornerstone of Pilgrim Congregational Church, 1899 -Lansing Public Library

"A Big One"-circa 1900-a great catch!! Photo from the Ziegler family.
-David R. Caterino

The hustle and bustle of Michigan Avenue, (ca. 1900's).
-Lansing Public Library

Union Depot on East Michigan Avenue, built in 1902, now Clara's Restaurant.
-State of Michigan Archives

Cherry Street School in 1905. "Sit up please!!"
-Lansing Public Library

Rare interior view of the Lansing Brewing Company located at 1301-1313 Turner Street. Amber Cream Beer was made here. -Rambo Collection

Students on sidewalk in front of Cedar Street School (ca. 1900's). -Lansing Public Library

Residence of R. E Olds (ca. 1912), 720 South Washington Avenue, built in 1902-03, house valued at $65,000 in 1937. -State of Michigan Archives

Lansing High School (ca. 1900). -Lansing Public Library

Looking south from the Michigan Avenue bridge, March 27, 1904. The Kalamazoo Street bridge is on the left, taken out by the flood.
-David R. Caterino

Travelling by boat on North Washington Avenue during the March 27, 1904 flood.
-Lansing Public Library

Intersection of River Street and Kalamazoo Street, March 1904 flood.
-State of Michigan Archives

Lansing High School 1905 football team.
A scrappy bunch! -Lansing Public Library

1906 Lansing High School girls basketball team.
-Lansing Public Library

1901 Lansing High School football team.
Outscored opponents 322-41. -Lansing Public Library

Townsend Street School (ca. 1900)
-State of Michigan Archives

Townsend Street School, 4th grade, September 1900. Miss Moots, teacher. First row: Schuyler Bertch, Junior Brooks, Leon Yakely, Katherine Deeg, Glen Brumm. Second row: Otto Schreiber, Clarence Olds, Robert Dewey, Grove Keith, Gene Avery. Third row: Frank Pitt, Ford Gunn, Craig Pattengill, Milburn Stabler. Fourth row: Vera Albright, Earl Holt, Alice Teller, Charles Long, Gladys Maltby. Fifth row: Havery Mullen, Lucile Titus, Claude Burnett.
-David R. Caterino

Cedar Street School, 8th grade, 1915.
-David R. Caterino

Turkish Baths at 106 W. Michigan Avenue. Fourth from left, George W. Gephart and on far right, owner Ed Reynolds (others unknown). -George D. Gephart

Michigan Avenue bridge looking south (ca. 1900's). -State of Michigan Archives

Waverly Park (ca. 1920). -State of Michigan Archives

Interior of Paul's Cigar Factory (1905), John Paul sits to the right of the desk. All cigars made there were rolled by hand. Paul's Cigar Factory was best known for making the Zack Chandler cigar. -George D. Gephart

Fire Station Number 3 (ca. 1900's).
-State of Michigan Archives

The Central Fire Station on the east side of Allegan Street (ca. 1900's), later the site of the first motorized vehicles owned by the Fire Department.
-State of Michigan Archives

Always serving the public, 1909 Department of Public Safety.
-Lansing Public Library

Lansing Auto Fire Department, 1912.
-State of Michigan Archives

Buck's Opera House built in 1873.
-Lansing Public Library

Depot at Trowbridge Junction, built in 1880.
-City of East Lansing

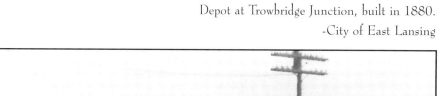

A coach from Porter's Transfer Line, taken in front of the Union Depot on E. Michigan Avenue (ca. 1908). -David R. Caterino

A line of Reo automobiles in front of the REO Motor Car Company Headquarters (ca. 1900's).
-State of Michigan Archives

George E. Lawrence and Sons bread delivery truck (ca. 1910).
-Lansing Public Library

In from Owosso, bringing many to Pine Lake (now known as Lake Lansing) and amusement park. The Lansing and Northeastern interurban was one of the few in the midwest to use a third rail system.
-Lansing Public Library

Lansing Fire Department members and their impressive truck at Station #3, 630 W. Hillsdale; 1914. Left to right; Forrest Perry, John Daily, Harry Begole, Claude F. Harrington (on top), Ned Dimminay, Earl Pettit, unknown.
-David R. Caterino

Lansing Vans (VanderVoorts Hardware) baseball team, 1925. Top row: (l to r) Louis Burgess, Bud Urquhort, Gordon Gallagher, Hallis Harkness, Gordon Rathburn, Larry Lung, Tom VanderVoort, Al Harryman, Jack Bates. Bottom row (l to r) Doc Shaw, Bill Mahoney, Monk Marvin, bat boy, Edward Planck, Frank Nowaczk, Joe Henry.
-David R. Caterino

John W. Tracy operated Tracy Auto Tire Repair Company at 526 E. Michigan Avenue around 1915. The Service Car promotes his 9582 phone number. John Tracy was an agent for Firestone Tire and Rubber Company.
-Rambo Collection

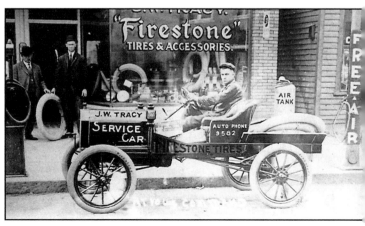

Egie D. Klock's barber shop at 1204 Turner Street, 1912.
-David R. Caterino

Haslett Park Station. Early Train Station in Haslett with work crew tipping their hats to the photographer (ca. 1910).
-Rambo Collection

A wonderful selection of lighting fixtures and supplies available in October, 1910 at the William F. Bohnet Electric Co., 118. E. Allegan. William Harris (left), W.F. Bohnet (right), Daphne Turner (front).
-M.S.U. Museum

William O. Thompson and son, Milton, 1910.
-David R. Caterino

Interior of grocery store at 316 S. Washington, Lansing in 1910; M.C. and E.V. Goosen, owners. Note Kellogg's Cereal display above counter.
-M.S.U. Museum

Pioneer Day Parade float, 1913. Standing is J. N. Bush, a local woodsman. The rifle in hand was made by Bush's father, an early pioneer.
-Lansing Public Library

Lansing Fried Cake Company trucks in front of Standard Chevrolet Sales, 419-423 East Michigan Avenue (ca. 1927).
-David R. Caterino

Otto Ziegler's Reo Speedwagon delivery truck for his hand-made cigar business.
-David R. Caterino

About 1930, Hurd's Delivery Car promotes three stores. The motto "You Can't Leave Dissatisfied" is displayed on the side of the car and the shop window advertises a special on shirts-just $1.95 each or three for $5.50.
-Rambo Collection

Madison Mills, flour mills, Christian R. Madison, proprietor, 220 Wall Street (ca. 1912). -State of Michigan Archives

Birds-eye view (ca. 1912) of Lansing the Capitol to Prospect Street. -Lansing Public Library

Tice Taylor, 1918, Lansing Pure Ice Company. -Lansing Public Library

St. Mary's Roman Catholic Church (under construction), 227 North Seymour Street, 1912. -State of Michigan Archives

S.H. Knox and Company 5 & 10 Store, South Washington Avenue looking southeast (ca. 1912). -State of Michigan Archives

200 block of North Washington Avenue, 1912. J. Stahl and Sons Hardware Store, Grinnel's Piano Shop, Gardner's Drug Store, H.L. Willson Harness and at far end is Buck's Opera House. -State of Michigan archives

115 North Walnut Street, built by Stowell and Marie Stebbins, 1914. Notice unique style of roofing. -Lansing Public Library

Ice Cream Stand at Pine Lake in Haslett. When spending a hot day at Pine Lake (now Lake Lansing) Davis & Co. of Lansing provided a mobile refreshment stand to patrons of the amusement park. The building in the background is the Pine Lake Casino. -Rambo Collection

Lansing's streetcars were used not only to transport people through town, but also for advertising purposes by local businesses. Lansing Public Library

Hyland's Garage-Magneto Specialist. Around 1913 Lee Hyland owned the Garage at 418 E. Franklin (later renamed Grand River). This large building also advertised Woodworth's Shoes and Stafford & Boos Real Estate. -Rambo Collection

Trinity African Methodist Episcopal Church,
109 North Pine Street (ca. 1920's).
-David R. Caterino

Manager Fred Kotz, with his
Toll Gate Cubs baseball team.
The team name derived from
a tollgate on Grand River
Avenue and Oakland.
-Lansing Public Library

Unidentified parade on
South Washington Avenue
at Allegan Street. Rouser's
Capital Drug Store at center
(ca. 1900).
-David R. Caterino

Lansing's first airstrip with participants looking on (ca. 1910's).
-Lansing Public Library

Knights Templer Conclave parade, North Washington Avenue at
Ottawa Street. May 31, 1921.
-David R. Caterino

Allen-Sparks Gas Light Company, manufacturers of gas lighting
systems, 420-422 East Michigan Avenue, 1912.
-State of Michigan Archives

Michigan Avenue,
facing west, with
trolley lines down
the middle of the
street (ca. 1920).
-David R. Caterino

The F.N. Arbaugh Company Department Store (ca. 1912), 401-409 S. Washington Avenue. Frank N. Arbaugh, President.
-State of Michigan Archives

(Lower Left) Christopher's Grocery, offered fresh produce and a place to sit (ca. 1920's).
-State of Michigan Archives

Display in the lobby of the Strand Theatre, 1921, South Washington Avenue.
-David R. Caterino

This unusual traffic tower was built by W. Bintz, City Engineer 1922. It was located at the busy intersection of Michigan Avenue and Washington Avenue.
-Rambo Collection

Traffic Tower, Lansing, M. Built by W. Bintz, City Eng. 1922. 231005e

Shiawassee St. Bridge
Lansing, Mich. Jan. 1-1923
Koss Construction Co., Builders
Photo by Leavenworth
5172

The street car platform in the middle of North Washington Avenue provided a precarious "safety zone" to wait for the next street car.
-**Rambo Collection

Shiawassee Street Bridge. A major construction zone or January 1, 1923. The photographer also snapped the Leavenworth car on right
-**Rambo Collectior

Vernon and Veronica Peters in a
goat-powered wagon in 1924.
-David R. Caterino

Fifth annual reunion of Union School, class of 1874. Potter Park, August 27, 1927.
-Lansing Public Library

Construction of Olds Hotel, July 2, 1925.
-Lansing Public Library

R.E. Olds is the first to register at his showcase Olds Hotel. Around 1926 Olds Hotel was built on the site of the Bijou Theater across from the State Capitol.
-**Rambo Collection

Cigar stand inside of lobby at Olds Hotel, 1927
-Lansing Public Library

Moores River Park swimming pool (ca. 1925).
-State of Michigan Archives

"Halloween at Violet Eckert's Home". Group of Fisher Body workers (ca. 1940's).
-David R. Caterino

Strand Theatre, October 8, 1930, Saturday matinee.
-Leavenworth Photography

Circus elephants advertise the American State Savings Bank, and promote 4% interest rates (ca. 1940's).
-**Rambo Collection

The Budweiser Clydesdale horses on parade on the 300 block of North Washington Avenue (ca. 1930's).
-David R. Caterino

A 1927 Buick Hearse parked out front of Gorsline and Runciman funeral home on Michigan Avenue where today the company and building are still living happily together with additions.
-Gorsline and Runciman

A view of the Lansing Dairy located at 518-530 North Cedar Street. There are horse drawn vehicles as well as motorized trucks (ca. late 1920's).
-Rambo Collection

A hand-made bomb on May 18, 1927 destroyed the Bath School, killing nearly 45 students and teachers while injuring many others. The bomb was planted by Andrew P. Kehoe and made front page news on many newspapers throughout the nation.
-Lansing Public Library

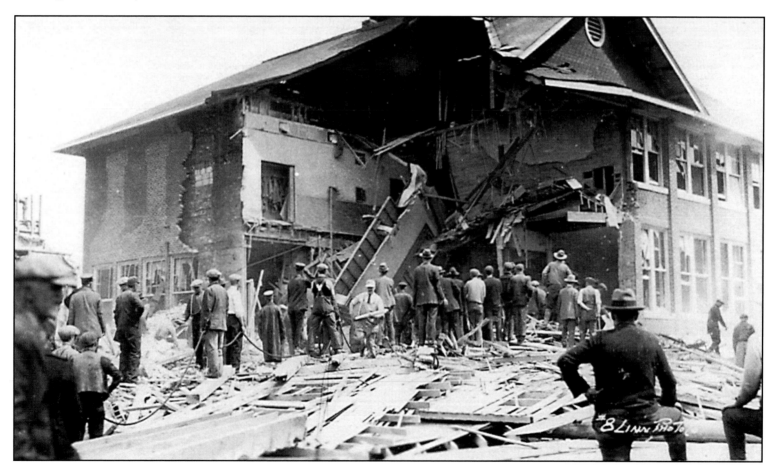

Palmer's Park at the north end of Pine Lake (now Lake Lansing), 1920's. This building burned in 1929 and was replaced by The Dell's Ballroom. The Dell's became Land's End in 1978 and was torn down in 1987 for condominiums.
-David R. Caterino

This is a photo of Lansing's first airmail. At the Lansing Airport, on Tuesday evening July 17, 1928 there were five sacks of mail that were taken from the field by pilot C.V. Pickup. Eastward bound mail was delivered in New York City Wednesday morning. Second from the left in the picture is Pilot Pickup, at his left is Walter G. Rogers, Lansing postmaster.
-Rambo Collection

A 1930's look down Michigan Avenue.
- Lansing Public Library

Say Cheese!! First anniversary of the Home Dairy Company cheese department on South Washington Avenue. -State of Michigan Archives

Michigan Mutual Liability Co. set up a "play by play" scoreboard on the side of their building so fans could follow the 1934 World Series. -Rambo Collection

World Series fans watch from the bleachers as the 6th inning "action" takes place in the 1934 Detroit vs. St. Louis game. -**Rambo Collection

Sealtest's new Big Top glasses filled with creamed cottage cheese, 28 cents. 1931 in-store display.
-Lansing Public Library

This photo shows the last load of people being lifted to the roof of the City National Bank Building at the corner of Michigan Avenue and Washington Avenue after its completion in the early 1930's. State Journal reporter Seth Whitmore is at the top of the right hand corner. He also rode the last beam of steel to the top of the Michigan National Tower when it was completed.
-Rambo Collection

Looking north, Lansing, Michigan; November 21, 1931.
-David R. Caterino

United State Post Office, completed in 1932. -Christman Company

The Kerns Hotel fire was December 11, 1934. Kerns Hotel was located 114-116 N. Grand Avenue. The 200 room hotel was often used by members of the State Legislature. Many guests were forced by the fire to jump into the Grand River at the rear of the Hotel or onto the pavement. The final list noted 34 dead and 40 injured.

-Lansing Public Library (left)

-**Rambo Collection (below)

Budd's Music House, 216 South Washington Avenue (ca. 1920's), a striking display of instruments.
-David R. Caterino

Capitol City Body Works tow truck, late 1930's. -David R. Caterino

Knapp's Department Store built in 1937 by the Christman Company.
-Chirstman Company

Store front of Sohn Linen Service 1935. Established in 1933 and still a thriving Lansing business today. Sohn

The Morlok Quadruplets, Edna, Wilma,
Sarah, and Helen. They were named for
Edward W. Sparrow Hospital
(E.W.S.H.). Born May 19, 1930 to
Sadie and Carl Morlok.
-David R. Caterino

Clem Sohn, the "bat man" who leapt from planes at 10,000 feet and soared over a
mile before releasing his parachute at 2,000 feet. Sohn was killed in a jump in
France. Photo circa 1930's.
-M.S.U. Museum

Lansing Dairy Company's Chevrolet delivery truck, 1929.
-David R. Caterino

Oldsmobile Old-Timers leaving for General Motor's "The March of Men and Motors" celebration in Detroit, January 11, 1939.
- David R. Caterino

Interior of Plaza Lunch, 400 South Washington Avenue (ca. 1940).
-David R. Caterino

Exterior of Plaza Lunch, 400 South Washington Avenue (ca. 1940).
-David R. Caterino

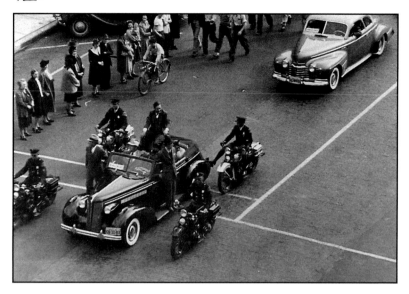

Presidential candidate Wendell Wilkie surrounded by security at a stop in Lansing (1940).
-David R. Caterino

Karl Kolsaw's band with seven members in 1940. David R. Caterino

On the steps of St. Mary's Church Bishop Albers with Knights of Columbus after service installing him as Lansing's first bishop 1937
-** Lillian Scieszka

1937-38
State League
basketball
champions,
the Michigan
State Highway
team.
-Lansing
Public Library

Chapter 3

WWII

Lansing Goes To War

1941 - 1946

When the United States entered World War II, the shock reached Lansing in several waves.

At home, rationing of many products, especially meat, sugar, and gas, affected every family every day.

At work, Lansing's industrial production was channeled into the "war effort." Factories, especially ones that built automobiles or provided parts for automobiles, became producers of war materiel for the Allies.

And on a personal level, the draft took away the men of Ingham County to fight in places most of them had never imagined. Of these, 468 never returned home. The losses are still being grieved.

No one could hide from this war, but the sacrifices brought victory.

Tin can drive ...everyone pitched in, (1942). -Lansing Public Library

Air raid warden does home check for black-out procedures, 1943.
-Lansing Public Library

First Aid, a part of Eastern High School war effort, October 21, 1942.
-Lansing Public Library

Lansing Control Center operation (ca. 1943).
-Lansing Public Library

Fourth of July Parade, WACs marching behind high school band (1942).
-Lansing Public Library

Mills Dry Goods Company employees, 1942. -Lansing Public Library

The Olds Girls and soldiers on roller skates at the Palomar Roller Rink on East Michigan Avenue, current location of the Silver Dollar Saloon.
-Jenny Hinkle

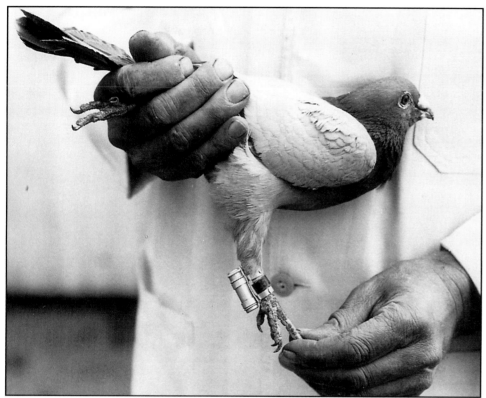

Close-up of homing pigeon with carrier, April 18, 1943.
-Lansing Public Library

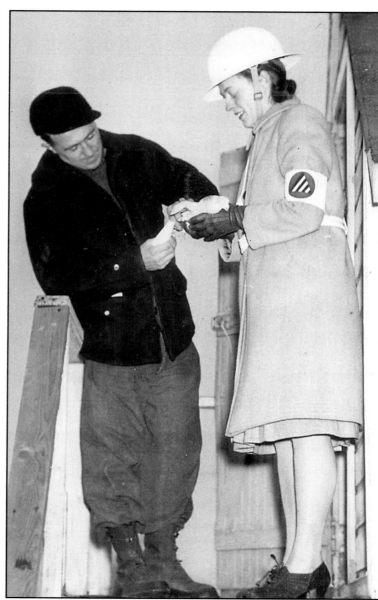

Ingham County
Defense Council
carrier pigeon as
messenger dur-
ing air raid drill.
-Lansing Public
Library

Neighborhood War Club
planning for increased
tin can collections,
autumn 1942.
-Lansing Public Library

Modern Air Raid Shelter, home of Lynn G.
Kellogg, 741 Cleo Street. Leonard Crispin
(Air Raid Warden).
-Lansing Public Library

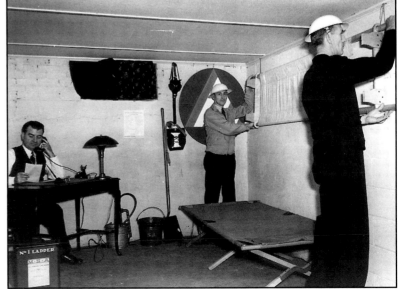

Civilian Defense Photo, children give tin cans for theatre tickets at Gladmer Theatre on North Washington Avenue (ca. 1942).
-Lansing Public Library

The night before tin can salvage, October 23, 1942.
-Lansing Public Library

Women's vocational class, Central High School; Frank Perne,
Instructor, July 26, 1942.
Lansing Public Library

Office of Dr. Grace Song Line,
tutoring Sgt. Culton L. Sturgill,
October 1, 1942.
-Lansing Public Library

Zone 6 Air Raid Wardens, March 2, 1943.
-Lansing Public Library

U.S.O party at Lansing YMCA, October 10, 1942.
-Lansing Public Library

Gas drill at
Michigan State
College, full
equipment and
ready in 40
seconds,
November 2,
1942.
-Lansing
Public Library

Instructional session on the mechanical workings of the wings of a World War II fighter plane.
-**Oldsmobile History Center

During of World War II, the civil air patrol in Lansing trained men in aviation fundamentals, taught flying and had civil duties to perform. Shown above are Lt. Carl W. Dalrymple (left), Lt. Harry Wilson in the cockpit, with a private (unknown) at the prop.
-Lansing Public Library

Lansing Eastern
High School
model airplane
building, October
12, 1942.
-Lansing Public
Library

Civil Defense checking passes to enter control center, September 16, 1942.
-Lansing Public Library

Our men go up Michigan Avenue. Fourth of July parade, 1942.
-Lansing Public Library

Volunteer workers during Lansing's first tin can collection, October 24, 1942.
-Lansing Public Library

Chapter 4

Beneath the Dome

The Capitol in the Capital City

For 150 years, its entire life, Lansing has been the seat of government for the State of Michigan. In the early days, the population of the state was small and legislators held sessions for a few weeks every other year.

Later, the State of Michigan became one of Lansing's largest employers, and much of Lansing's stability comes from the presence of the State in its City.

Legislators have held sessions in two capitol buildings in Lansing. The first, a frame Greek Revival structure built in 1847, was used for thirty-two years.

The second capitol, built of limestone in 1879 at a cost of $1,505,000.00, was recently restored to national acclaim. It is Lansing's - and Michigan's - finest building.

Second Capitol (built in 1847) in the foreground, new Capitol in background (ca. 1880's). -Capitol Archives

View of Capitol down Michigan Ave. during construction (1877). -Capitol Archives

Downtown Lansing as seen from E. Kalamazoo St. bridge, 1877. -Capitol Archive

Dr. William W. Root, Mason, 1881;
Michigan House of Representatives.
-David R. Caterino

Senate and House janitors (ca. 1881).
-David R. Caterino

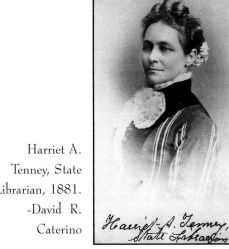

Harriet A.
Tenney, State
Librarian, 1881.
-David R.
Caterino

S.H. Carmer, 1881, of Carmer
Parmalee Company, member of
Michigan House of Representatives,
from 1st District, Ingham County.
-David R. Caterino

Capitol just after completion (1880); building in foreground
owned by a janitor in the State Republican Building.
-Capitol Archives

Capitol dominates
Lansing's skyline, 1887.
-Capitol Archives

State House of Representatives
Chamber, 1888
-Capitol Archives

Early look at newly completed Capitol. (ca.1880).
-Capitol Archives

(lower left) Members of
the Michigan House of
Representatives, 1885.
-Capitol Archives

Prince's Military Band on the
Capitol steps (ca. 1890's).
-Rambo Collection

Michigan Senate on steps of Capitol, 1889.

-David R. Caterino

(upper right) Chamber of the House of Representatives, 1899.

-Capitol Archives

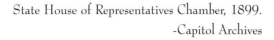

State House of Representatives Chamber, 1899.

-Capitol Archives

A decorated Capitol awaits the arrival of President Teddy Roosevelt. Notice his picture inset on banner midway up center of Capitol. May, 1907.
-Capitol Archives

Group of soldiers on Capitol steps.
World War I era.
-David R. Caterino

-Capitol Archives

"HUMAN FLY" MR GARDNER
PLACING FLAG ON
CAPITOL DOME LANSING, MICH.
OCT. 10, 1917

LINN PHOTO CO

-Rambo Collection

Lansing's First Zeppelin.
Goodyear. "Puritan" Sept. 26, 1929.
Halbert.

Governor Albert E. Sleeper signs the women's suffrage bill, 1920.
-Capitol Archives

Celebration on Capitol steps of Michigan Agricultural College's shutout football victory over Wabash, November 16, 1912.
-David R. Caterino

On steps of Capitol (ca. 1920's) Memorial Day, citizens pay homage to those who have fallen. These steps were the sight of many historic events and everyday gatherings.
-Capitol Archives

Ferguson Lindy Willis poses on cannon in front of Capitol (ca. 1929).
-Capitol Archives

Capitol rotunda, 2nd floor, Gallery of the Governors.
-Capitol Archives

Furniture City (Grand Rapids) Band on Capitol steps, 1912. -Capitol Archives

Michigan Motorbus Association on Capitol steps, 1940.
-Capitol Archives

Former Michigan Governor G. Mennen Williams admires
the State Flag. Governor Williams served from 1949 to
1960. His nickname was "Soapy" and his trademark was
his green and white polka-dot bow tie.
-Rambo Collection

Ornate light fixture
within the Capitol.
-Dianne Gnass

Capitol Building's Centennial Celebration, 1979. -Capitol Archives

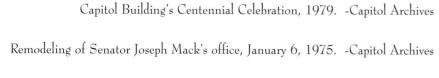

Remodeling of Senator Joseph Mack's office, January 6, 1975. -Capitol Archives

A workman restores the outside of the Capitol dome, 1992. -Capitol Archives

Restoration of Capitol Dome, 1992. -Al Kamuda/Detroit Free

Present interior view
of the dome, May, 1997.
-Dianne Gnass

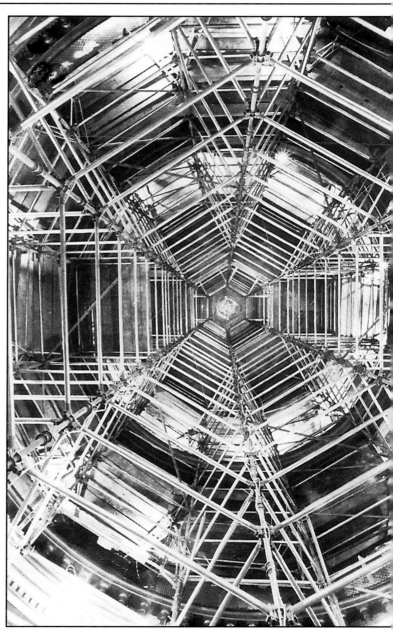

Capitol dome
under restoration,
December, 1990.
-Capitol Archives

West side of Capitol Building, spring 1997 -Fowler

"The Greatest", Muhammad Ali "throws a left jab" while visiting the Michigan House of Representatives in the spring of 1997. Following his retirement Ali lived for many years in Berrien Springs, Michigan. -David Trumpie

A picturesque night photo of the Capitol, taken July 13, 1997 from top of Michigan National Bank Tower. -Jason Hamelin

May, 1997 -Fowler

Chapter 5

On the Banks of the Red Cedar

M.A.C. to M.S.C. to M.S.U.

In 1857, Michigan Agricultural College, the first land-grant college in the nation, opened in the countryside near Lansing. Its mission was to train young men in the science of agriculture. Engineering, natural sciences, philosophy, and literature were required courses.

After a rousing start, enrollment dropped to 48 students during the Civil War and the legislature considered closing the college. Three men who helped save it held long tenure at the college: Robert Kedzie, Chemistry, 1863-1902; William Beal, Botany, 1870-1910; and T.C. Abbot, English, 1858-85, and President, 1864-85.

Women were admitted in 1871; "women's courses" were initiated in 1896.

Enrollment grew to nearly 15,000 when the GIs came to campus after WWII. "Temporary" quonset huts were used for classrooms and housing.

Today, with much expanded program choices, enrollment at Michigan State University stands at over 40,000. MSU is nationally famous for the beauty of its campus.

State of Michigan Archives

M.A.C. Students watching the Red Cedar River ice floes in 1904-5 from the railroad bridge that led to the old university power plant. -M.S.U. Museum

Professor Herman Klock Vedder, Civil Engineering Department at M.A.C., circa 1900.
-M.S.U. Museum

In 1884 the United State Post Office was established at Michigan Agricultural College. R.G. Baird, Postmaster. Ira Howard Butterfield, Secretary of M.A.C. and to Mr. Butterfield's left, Clenton Butterfield.
-City of East Lansing

The Botany Class at Michigan Agricultural College in 1885 has a majority of women students. The professor standing to the far right is Frank S. Kedzie.
-Rambo Collection

Wells Hall at Michigan Agricultural College (ca. 1900), built in the 1870's and destroyed by fire on February 11, 1905.
-David R. Caterino

Presenting the 1885 graduates of Botany Class at Michigan Agricultural College. Seated in the middle is Professor Frank S. Kedzie.
-Rambo Collection

Jamming to the tunes of M.A.C. the
talented trio (ca. 1900's).
-M.S.U. Museum

This photo is in the 1911 Michigan Agricultural
College Wolverine Yearbook, titled "Old and New
Captains of '08-'09".
-David R. Caterino

M.A.C. baseball team "Spring Term 1909".
-David R. Caterino

Michigan Agricultural College vs. University of Michigan, 1908 a rare complete ticket and real photo postcard of the memorable scoreless tie.
-David R. Caterino

Michigan Agricultural College basketball team, 1910.
-David R. Caterino

(below)
Postcards produced for
Michigan Agricultural
College's semi-centennial
in 1907. President
Theodore Roosevelt gave a
speech at M.A.C.
-David R. Caterino

The famous photo of R.E. Olds driving President Teddy Roosevelt east on Michigan Avenue May 31, 1907. Joining these historic figures are M.A.C. President Jonathan Snyder in backseat and next to Olds is Roosevelt's secretary William Loeb.
-State of Michigan Archives

Teddy's going to teach
me the new way to spell
at LANSING MICH.
MAY 31
ROOSEVELT DAY
PHONETIC SPELLING BOOK
BIG STICK

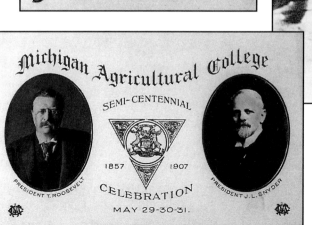

Michigan Agricultural College
SEMI-CENTENNIAL
1857 — 1907
CELEBRATION
MAY 29-30-31.
PRESIDENT T. ROOSEVELT
PRESIDENT J.L. SNYDER

Agricultural short course students at M.S.C. in the 1930's.
-M.S.U. Museum

Agricultural Hall, M.A.C., 1908.
-Christman Company

Agricultural Hall, Michigan
Agricultural College (ca. 1909),
housed the early agricultural
faculty and staff.
-State of Michigan Archives

Sites of Michigan
Agricultural College
(ca. 1910's).
-State of Michigan
Archives

Annual barbeque at M.A.C.-This annual special event was prepared by the Sophomore class and featured juicy ox sandwiches, with visitors requested to bring a tin cup for fresh apple cider. (ca. 1919).
-M.S.U. Museum

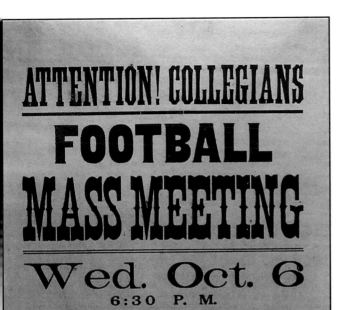

ATTENTION! COLLEGIANS

FOOTBALL

MASS MEETING

Wed. Oct. 6

6:30 P. M.

Armory

The following speakers will make three-minute speeches:

DEAN SHAW	DEAN BISSELL	PROF. BAKER
JACK BOWDITCH	COACH BREWER	CAPT. McKENNA

YELLS

(Locomotive yell.)

I. Rah!—Rah!—Rah!
Uz, Uz, Uz.
M. A. C.—Tiger.

II. Osky-wow-wow—Skinny-
wow-wow.
Skinny-wow-wow-wow-
wow-wow.

III. Goodness,—Gracious,—Mercy me.
Wabash and old M. A. C.,
Willy Willy Wad! Hitem with
a Cod!
Wabash!   Wabash!   Oh my
Gracious!

IV. Rat-a-ta-thrat! ta-thrat!
ta-thrat!
Terrors to lick! to lick! to lick!
Kick-a-ba-ba! Kick-a-ba-ba!
M. A. C.! M. A. C.! Rah!-Rah!
Rah!

V. M. A. C.
U-Rah! U-Rah!
M. A. C.
U-Rah! U-Rah! Hoorah!
Hoorah!
M. A. C.! Rah! Tiger!

VI. Hold! M. A. C.! Hold! M. A. C.!
(repeat.)

VII. Block that kick! Block that kick!
(repeat.)

Bring your voices and turn 'em loose.

Co-eds especially invited.   Everybody welcome, even sub-faculty.

THE BAND WILL BE THERE.

(BE SURE AND SAVE FOR FUTURE USE)

Lawrence & Van Buren Printing Co

FRESHMEN!

COUNT YOUR DAYS

Considering Your Undesired and
Abominable Appearance, WE,
the Class of 1916, Will Eradi-
cate Your Goodfornothin' Car-
cases from our Sanctum on

DOOMSDAY
OCTOBER 4, '13

"Our   Short and Snappy"

OUR SYMBOL— GORE

Signed, M. A. C. Class of 1916

(Far left) Rare football mass meeting broadside at Michigan Agricultural College, October 6, 1909, designed to increase enthusiasm for the team.
-David R. Caterino

Copy (on photo postcard) of a poster for the M.A.C. Junior-Freshmen football game, 1913.
-David R. Caterino

Scenes from 1912, Michigan Agricultural College.
-State of Michigan Archives

1913 Michigan Agricultural College football team. Gideon Smith, first black football player at M.A.C. -David R. Caterino

M.A.C. Students at banquet, circa 1915.
M.S.U. Museum

"A Jerked Beef Party" on Campus in
1911 at M.A.C., with students enjoying a tasty treat. Notice student in
back with bottle on his forehead!
-M.S.U. Museum

Members of the 1918 M.A.C. Student
Army Training Corps, where 500 soldiers
were sent to the campus for training in
truck maintenance and operation. The
truck squad rolls past the old Dairy
Student Building.
-M.S.U. Museum

Construction of Beaumont Tower (1928).
-State of Michigan Archives

The College Book Store across from the Michigan Agricultural
College campus on Grand River Avenue, 1910.
-City of East Lansing

Swartz Creek Band, asked to perform for the annual police and fireman's banquet at the Olds Hotel in Lansing. They couldn't be excused from classes in 1928 for band practice, so police arranged for the band members to be "arrested" during class and hauled away in a patrol wagon to the banquet!
-M.S.U. Museum

A serpentine line of students winds its way down Grand River Avenue following Michigan Agricultural College's huge victory over Michigan in baseball, May 24, 1926
-City of East Lansing

Swartz Creek Band at M.S.C.; originally formed in 1920, this photo was taken later at Mulliken (see photo above) -M.S.U. Museum

M.S.U. Students in mid-1950's testing milk
in Dairy Science Building on campus.
-M.S.U. Museum

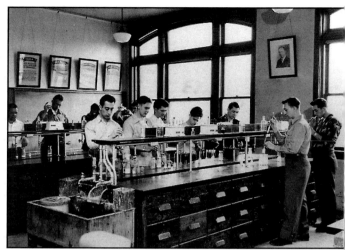

The mid-fifties brought at Michigan State
University drastic changes over a three-year
period to Macklin Field. These changes
were directly attributed to the great success
of Spartan football during the early 1950's.
-Lansing Public Library

M.S.U. Band member Nelson
Brown, looking at the 1954 Official
Rose Bowl program, making plans
for his 1956 trip to Pasadena.
-M.S.U. Museum

Michigan State University, Beaumont Tower (ca. 1950's).
State of Michigan Archives

Spartan boosters preparing to board plane for flight to
football game against Wisconsin, October 29, 1955.
-Lansing Public Library

Drum section of the M.S.U. Marching Band in 1962.
-M.S.U. Museum

Horn section of the M.S.C. Band
in the early 1950's.
-M.S.U. Museum

George J. Perles, storied football Head Coach at Michigan State University being carried off the field in Ann Arbor following the Spartans 19-7 victory over the Michigan Wolverines. He restored glory to the Spartan football program when he returned the Spartans to the Rose Bowl in 1988 and during his tenure, he won more games than any coach in Spartan football history.
-Michigan State Sports Information

Chapter 6

Oldsmobile

A Century of Excellence

In 1897, Ransom E. Olds organized the Olds Motor Vehicle Co., the first company formed solely for the manufacture of the automobile. A new company, the Olds Motor Works, was lured to Detroit in 1899, but after a fire in the plant, Olds was induced to return to Lansing, and "Oldsmobile" became a major name in the industry.

With races and publicity stunts, Olds gained a national reputation for the auto. He also designed the first progressive assembly system, which Henry Ford adapted several years later.

By 1904 when R.E. Olds left the company, about 8000 Curved Dash Runabouts had been produced, small cars selling for about $650.

Olds Motor Works shifted to the production of larger cars, and in 1908 joined General Motors.

Oldsmobile has long been one of Lansing's largest employers and is world famous for its "Rocket" engine, Hydra-Matic transmission, and front-wheel drive Toronado, all built in Lansing.

Oldsmobile History Center

Ransom E. Olds at the controls of his first internal-combustion engine vehicle, with Frank Clark next to him.
-Oldsmobile History Center

The 1905 Oldsmobile Light Delivery Wagon. -Oldsmobile History Center

A busy Oldsmobile assembly line in 1934.
**Oldsmobile History Center

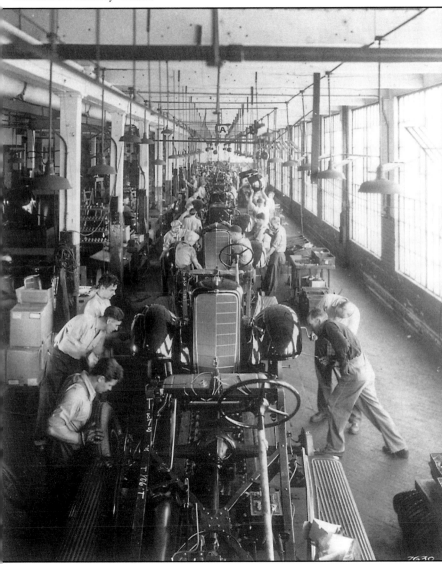

Oldsmobile's Product Engineering Department, June 6, 1931.
-**Oldsmobile History Center

Oldsmobile constructed its new Administration Building in 1930. The building would serve as the company's headquarters for more than 35 years.
-**Oldsmobile History Center

General Manager C. L. McCuen and General Sales Manager D.E. Ralston took over the reins of Oldsmobile in 1933; this 1940 Custom Cruiser four-door was the one-millionth car produced under their leadership. -**Oldsmobile History Center

A group of gun school trainees march down Olds Avenue. Oldsmobile helped to train many of the soldiers who would ultimately use the materiel produced by the company.
**Oldsmobile History Center

The GM Juniors performed a half-hour radio program on Lansing's WJIM-AM.
-**Oldsmobile History Center

Rockets built in the Oldsmobile plant are inspected for accuracy.
-Oldsmobile History Center

Oldsmobile sponsored a float during a
war-time Lansing parade.
-**Oldsmobile History Center

The General Motors Girls' advertisement for a 10th
Anniversary Dance held March 10th 1943.
Proceeds benefited War Activities.
-Oldsmobile History Center

Gun training at Oldsmobile concluded with the "blindfold test," where students had to disassemble and reassemble a gun while blindfolded. The record was 42 seconds! -**Oldsmobile History Center

Oldsmobile's industrial safety program had its roots in World War II. A plant protection officer shows employees how to use a gas mask.
-**Oldsmobile History Center

Veteran tries out his new wheels specially designed by Oldsmobile to serve his needs.
-Oldsmobile History Center.

Oldsmobile manufactured an array of artillery shells during World War II, ranging in size from 75mm to 155mm (the latter shown at far right).
-**Oldsmobile History Center

Lt. Byron Abbott shows some of the Olds keys that were collected for scrap metal. Conservation took on extreme importance.
-**Oldsmobile History Center

World War II required significant amounts of money, both at home and abroad. The Ingham County war fund drive combined the needs for many of the charitable organizations into one pledge. A banner in the plant encourages workers to buy bonds.
-**Oldsmobile History Center

Oldsmobile keeps 'em firing! The company shows the community the war materiel manufactured at this outdoor exhibit. **Oldsmobile History Center

Down and dirty for Olds workers in their continual production of war time needs for the troops. -Oldsmobile History Center.

Packaging a 75mm cannon for shipment was common routine for many Olds workers in 1942. -** Oldsmobile History Center.

Olds workers carefully inspect the new line as they have for decades. (1942). -Oldsmobile History Center.

Front ends assembled in Building
75-Olds Main Plant-1949.
-**Oldsmobile History Center

Assembly line
production of
artillery shells.
(1942)
-Oldsmobile
History Center

Red Cross volunteers
receive donations in
aiding war time efforts.
Advertisement
encourages people to
"Keep your Red Cross
at his side," during
this 1942 fund drive.
-** Oldsmobile History
Center.

General Douglas MacArthur greets employees at Olds who had served under him in combat, May 15, 1952.   -**Oldsmobile History Center.

The five-millionth Oldsmobile, a 1955 98 Holiday sedan, was built on July 27, 1955. General Manager Jack Wolfram is at the wheel, with Bob Rollis, general manufacturing manager, about to get in the back seat.
-**Oldsmobile History Center

General Manager Jack Wolfram looks on as Jimmy Stewart and his wife check out a car the the 1954 Motorama.
-**Oldsmobile History Center

Vice President Richard M. Nixon came to Lansing and was whisked away in a 1954 Olds 98 sedan with his name on the side.
.**Oldsmobile History Center

An aerial view of the vast main plant, (1959). -**Oldsmobile History Center

Constructed in 1919, the Olds water tower had become part of the plant's skyline. But with the advent of large diesel pumps, the gravity-pressure system was no longer needed, and the 100,000 gallon tank was removed a piece at a time in 1971.
-**Oldsmobile History Center

To encourage safety, posters encouraging seat-belt use were distributed to dealers and hung inside the plant. Shown holding a poster in 1961 are (l to r) Herb Stewart, Dee Smith, and Marlene Farhat.
-**Oldsmobile History Center

In the sixties, striping was a popular option; R. Pearl is shown plying his art to a 1967 Toronado.
-**Oldsmobile History Center

As part of the 75th anniversary, I-496 was renamed Olds Freeway. State Senator Phil Pittinger unveils the new sign August 21, 1972. -**Oldsmobile History Center

Air cushion restraints (later known as air bags) were offered in a variety of GM cars in 1973. The first, a Toronado, rolled off the line on November 29,1973. Ed Cole tries out the air cushion restraint test device. - ** Oldsmobile History Center

Oldsmobile celebrated its 75th anniversary on August 21, 1972. Lansing held a huge parade with floats sponsored by many companies with a reviewing stand in front of the Capitol. -**Oldsmobile History Center

A sad day in Olds history when, in April of 1990, when the last Rocket V-8 engine was built. Employees on the engine assembly line signed the engine which was donated to the R.E. Olds Transportation Museum.
**Oldsmobile History Center

Chapter 7

Lansing Comes Home

Baby Boomers

1947 - 1964

In the 20 years after WWII, Lansing's triple base of government, industry and education continued to develop. State government increased with the population, Oldsmobile and REO plants met demand with high production rates, and Michigan State University expanded each year. In 1957 Lansing Community College was started, reflecting a new approach to higher education.

This same growth created the need for more housing and city services, more retail establishments, and even fast food: the first McDonald's opened in Lansing in 1957. In 1954, Frandor Shopping Center opened, and WKAR-TV began broadcasting.

While Lansing has had an airport since 1926, when air travel was in its infancy, following WWII passenger service increased dramatically.

Lansing was surrounded by quiet towns; only East Lansing could be considered a suburb. The focus of the growth was still within Lansing.

Emil's Place on East Michigan Avenue, Emil DeMarco (center). -Emil's Restaurant

Borden's Ice Cream Company truck backed up to a tent, providing concessions for the Ringling Brothers, Barnum and Bailey Circus. Some of their hats promote "Coca Cola 10¢ Pay No More." They are also selling Cracker Jack and Ice Cream (ca. 1940's). -Rambo Collection

Parade scene in front of Princess Shop (115 N. Washington Avenue), W.T. Grant Store in process of being built (117-123 N. Washington Avenue). To the far right is the Tussing Building (ca. early 1950's) -Norm Shaver/Rambo Collection

Night scene of East Michigan Avenue from front of Capitol Building; Hotel Olds on right (ca. 1940's).
-Lansing Public Library

Howard K. Finch (Uncle Howdy) with guest on WJIM Radio. Late 1940's.
-David R. Caterino

Bailey School (fourth grade) in East Lansing.
Note at left twin sister's, 1944.
-City of East Lansing

East Lansing High School's boys
basketball team, (ca. 1940's).
-East Lansing Public Library

Looking east on Allegan Street toward Washington and Grand Avenues.
The Hollister Building on the left is Lansing's oldest office building, completed in 1893. (ca. 1948)
Lansing Public Library

In February, 1951, the State Office
Building, home of the State Library, was set
on fire. The act of arson caused damage and
destruction to the building, state records, and
thousands of library books
-Rambo Collection

Firemen remove injured from State Building fire, 1951. -State of Michigan Archives

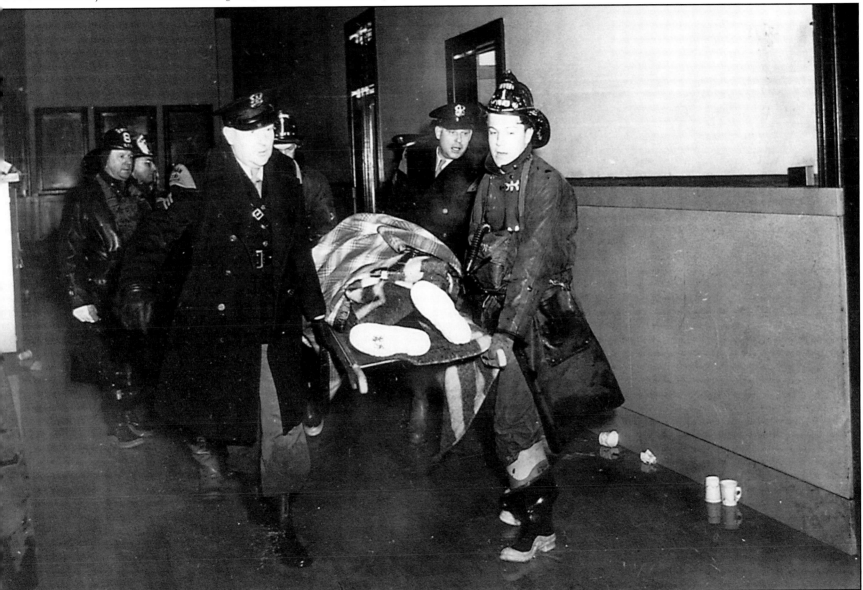

On May 15, 1952, General Douglas
MacArthur arrives in Lansing.
-**Oldsmobile History Center

In an emotional moment, General
Douglas MacArthur consoles the
wife and daughter of a fallen soldier
during his May 1952 Lansing visit.
-**Oldsmobile History Center

Olivia Davis Letts and husband Richard Letts have had tremendous impact on the Lansing community (1994 photo - lower left).
Olivia was Lansing's first black elementary school teacher hired in 1951. Richard shown here organizing yet another event for
Lansing's youth in 1953 at the Lincoln Community Center. They represent pillars in the Greater Lansing community.
Letts Family Collection

Frandor Shopping Center built in 1954. Michigan's second oldest shopping center. Wrigley's Super Market in location of current Kroger's.
-David R. Caterino

A unique partial view of the Capitol as Lansing continues to undergo facelifts (ca. 1950's).
-Matthew Blackledge

Howard Sober, Inc., pioneers in the auto haulaway business with a load of 1956 Oldsmobiles.
-David R. Caterino

Students from Michigan School for the Blind, (1955). -Margaret Schrepfer

Lansing Community College opens its doors in 1957.
-Lansing Public Library

A popular hamburger joint, Kewpee's, serves customers on the sidewalk along East Grand River Avenue in East Lansing. It's now Jacobson's Department Store. (ca. late 1950's)
-East Lansing Public Library

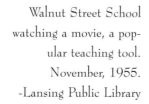

Walnut Street School watching a movie, a popular teaching tool. November, 1955.
-Lansing Public Library

School's out!! Pattengill Junior High School 1956 -Lansing Public Library

Looking westward from the intersection of East Michigan Avenue and West Grand River Avenue in East Lansing (current site of a 7-11 store), May 13, 1957.
-City of East Lansing

East Lansing Police Department officer directs bumper to bumper traffic along Grand River Avenue, 1957.
-City of East Lansing

East Lansing's Fire Department displays some of its equipment during the Golden Anniversary parade, June 8, 1957.
-City of East Lansing

Election Day, 1956. East Lansing's new voting machine.
City of East Lansing

The annual East Lansing Kiwanis Club's community chicken barbeque, June 8, 1957.
-City of East Lansing

Looking west on Michigan Avenue to an illuminated Capitol Dome.
-Lansing Public Library

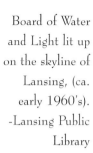

Board of Water and Light lit up on the skyline of Lansing, (ca. early 1960's).
-Lansing Public Library

A new home for Story Oldsmobile (1959), corner of Michigan Avenue and Morgan Street.
-Story Oldsmobile.

Spring day, 1957, Lansing Community Center playground.
-Lansing Public Library

April 26, 1962 Mt. Hope School sixth grade Safety Patrol Squad. -Lansing Public Library

Zonta International and Santa deliver poinsettias
to those less privileged at Christmas time (1960).
-Lansing Public Library

Holmes School, Mrs. Van Atta's kindergarten class (1961), First row: (l to r) Jimmy Bott,
Darcel Jackson, Julie Peters, Celeste Thompson, Timmy Holland, Donna James, Jimmy
Peeper, Steven Bush, Steven Farr. Second row: Scott Miller, Kim Carney, Bobby Maxey,
Cindy Lewis, Ann Volz, Mike Yowaish, Andrea Spata. Third row: Gene Hendershott,
John Van Derske, Gregory Bower, Ricky Sparks, Ronnie Albert, Tommy Bryde, Carlo
Tombelli, Rosie Sigourney, David Curtiss.
- Lansing Public Library

League of Women Voters march down Grand River to demonstrate their position on voting (ca. 1964).
-City of East Lansing

1965 shop class, Eastern High School.
-Lansing Public Library

East Lansing Fire Department Truck (ca.1960's).
-City of East Lansing

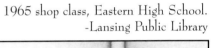

Chapter 8

Coming of Age

Moving Towards the Next Millennium

1965 - 1997

For thirty years, the population has grown most outside the city, changing the face of the entire Lansing area.

Large shopping malls opened outside of town on the west and east sides. New housing bloomed in the suburbs and countryside. New types of businesses diversified the economic base. The Lansing area is developing a regional approach to such growth.

In Downtown Lansing, Riverfront Park opened in 1976 on land cleared along the Grand River. The RiverWalk now runs from the Turner-Dodge House to MSU. Theaters and museums have grown. Lansing Community College created a campus within the city.

Recently, Downtown Lansing also has seen the restoration of the 1879 Capitol, and the building of the Michigan Historical Center, the Lansing Center, and the Baseball Stadium.

And as people develop urban revival attitudes, they are reclaiming urban houses and neighborhoods again.

Such changes will direct our future.

Fowler

Clarence Nolan Bartow, Lansing's well-known violin maker (ca. 1960's).
-David R. Caterino

Bundling up at the community nursery, 1966.
-Lansing Public Library

"Stay in the cross-walk". East Lansing school crossing, 1960's.
-City of East Lansing

Children playing at the daycare with home made boats, Summer of 1966.
-Eugenia McCoubrey

Elementary school students practice a school bus evacuation drill at the Spartan Village School, March 1979.
-City of East Lansing

Sunday School at First Presbyterian Church 1967. First Presbyterian was Lansing's first charter to organize in 1847. Early services then were held sometimes in a horse barn which affectionally came to be called 'God's Barn'.
-The First Presbyterian Church.

Lansing Community College's Turner House, when still a museum. Note the construction of the Dart Building in Rear. -Lansing Community College

Pot luck dinners were very popular at many Lansing area churches. This one was held at First Presbyterian Church in the 1970's. -The First Presbyterian Church.

Bicycle built for two.
Motor powered tricycle
transports this elderly
couple around their
Lansing neighborhood.
(ca. 1977).
-Lansing Public Library

Fourth of July 1976, Bicentennial of the United States. Children celebrate with commemorative flags at Lansing parade.
-Lansing Public Library

Dominic Quintela 10, loads back of a pick-up truck after the winds blew from the 1978 REO fire toward her relatives home.
-Lansing Public Library

One of thousands of demonstrations held on the Capitol steps. This one held in 1977 was run by the National Organization for Women.
-Lansing Public Library

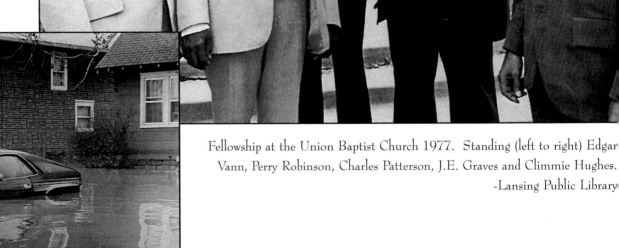

This vehicle definitely will not start! The flood of 1978 created scenes like this all over Lansing.
-Lansing Public Library

Fellowship at the Union Baptist Church 1977. Standing (left to right) Edgar Vann, Perry Robinson, Charles Patterson, J.E. Graves and Climmie Hughes.
-Lansing Public Library

Checking in at the Lansing Capitol City Airport June 27, 1974. North Central Airlines no longer operates.
-Capitol City Airport

(lower left) Reo Motors building in July 1979 shortly before the building was demolished.
-Jay L. Hinkle

Second Hand Rose- Customer on chair in front of store at 431 E. Michigan Avenue (ca. early 1980's), where Oldsmobile Park is now located.
-David R. Caterino

Feline Primate Building, renovated in 1989, at Potter Park Zoo.
-Potter Park Zoo

Michigan Library and Historical Center, a state of the art
facility, (1997).
-Jason Hamelin

Greater Lansing Symphony Orchestra conducted by Gustav Meier, January 28, 1989. Established in 1929 under the artist direction of Izler Solomon, the GLSO has evolved into a professional metropolitan orchestra that has provided the Lansing area with many years of musical enjoyment.
-Greater Lansing Symphony Orchestra

Built in 1931, the original home of City National Bank, at the corner of Washington Avenue and East Michigan Avenue, is now home to Comerica Bank, (1996).
-**Comerica Bank

Downtown Lansing trumpets its Sesquicentennial Celebration, (1997).
-Fowler

Young Alec playing in one of Lansing's beautiful Autumn afternoons. (1996)
-Dianne Gnass

Jackson National Life Insurance Company's headquarters as it appears today. The view is looking east. Jackson National Life is Michigan's largest life insurance company.
-Kim Kauffman

A word from President William Jefferson Clinton to the Greater Lansing community. President Clinton spoke on M.S.U. campus August 27, 1996 enroute to Chicago for the Democratic National Convention. -Fowler

Tom Merrifield Jr. and Tom III. swinging in Durant Park on corner of Saginaw and Washington spring 1997. -Fowler

Grand River Dam on a beautiful 1997 spring day. -Fowler

The Lansing community led by Mayor David Hollister "Make it happen" by adding Oldsmobile Park in 1996 between Cedar Street and Larch Street. The park is a major league facility for minor league players.
-Fowler

Take me out to the ballgame! James Riley Jr. with wife Mary and 4 year old son Jackson, entering Oldsmobile Park. (1997)
-Fowler

Sharme'l Hopkins relaxes out in front of Peanut Shop on South Washington Avenue. (1997)
-Fowler

Morgan B. Ford home built by Ford in 1880. Corner of Pine Street and Ionia Street. Restored in 1958 by realtor Marguerite Moore. (1997). -Fowler

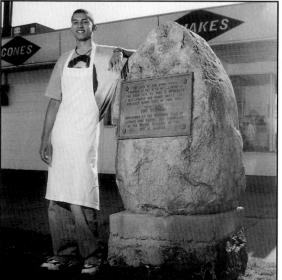

North Grand River Avenue plaque on boulder commemorates site of first Lansing home built by pioneer John Burchard. 1997 Eastern High School Graduate Gabriel Smiley works at Tate's Freeze, in background. (1997). -Fowler

Ed's Bar with owner Paul Czubak on Grand River Avenue in Old Lansing. Paul's grand-father and father passed this establishment on from original ownership in 1943. Previously building was site of Fortino's Confection. P.S. Paul was born upstairs. (1997). -Fowler

The River Walk a popular setting for jogging, walking and general relaxation the River Walk with Board of Water and Light in background. (1997).
-Fowler

Michigan, Michigan April 27, 1847 reprint of original postmark. (1997).
-Greater Lansing Historical Society

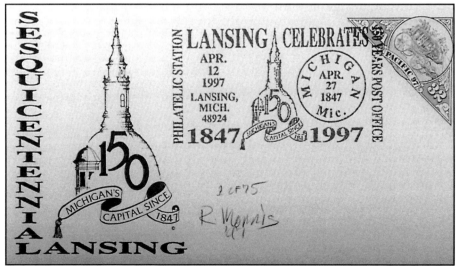

The Christian Basketball Infantry Corps "getting in shape," on west side of Capitol, (1997). -Fowler.

Thank You

Without the tremendous contributions of the following people and organizations this book would not have been possible.

David R. Caterino

City of East Lansing: Edna M. Poore

East Lansing Public Library

Lansing Public Library: Peg Shaub

Leavenworth Photographics: Roger Boettcher

Michigan State University Museum: Val R. Berryman,
Angela Riedel

Oldsmobile History Center: Helen J. Earley

Rambo Collection: Martha Rambo

State Capitol Archives: Kerry K. Chartkoff
Jerry Lawyler

State of Michigan Archives: John Curry,
Leroy Barnett

The First Presbyterian Church: Ardelle Boettcher,
Aleen T. Cross

Michael E. Unsworth

Kevin Fowler, a St. Louis, Missouri native, came to Lansing in 1979 to attend MSU. He has pursued photography as a career for the last 4 years. Fowler's contributions to *Through the Years*, include photography throughout and copy work on many old photos.

Thank You

The following citizens and businesses contributed photos and captions from 'throughout the years' for this publication.

Courtney Antcliff
Doug Barry
Helen Black
Mr. & Mrs. Matthew Blackledge
Scott Blotto
Skyler Boskal
Donald Canfield
Ann Chaffee
Marilyn Culpepper
Comerica Inc.
Garnet Chappell
Doug Cooper
Francis M. Coryell
Joseph Cullen
Eleanore DeMarco
Mark Dunn
Emil's Restaurant
Pauly Feller
Lisa Marie Gagarin
George D. Gephart
Barry Gibson
Gordy G. Gibson

Cullen Gnass
Dianne Gnass
Gorsline-Runciman Co.
Greater Lansing Association of Realtors
Greater Lansing Symphony Association
Paul M. Grotelueschen
H.G. Christman Company
Jason Hamelin
R. Jon Harpst
Patrick Hegarty
Jenny & J.L. Hinkle
Randy Hudson
Jackson National Life
Carol Keller-Webster
Dirk Koetter
Lansing Community College
Lansing Capitol City Airport
Lansing Regional Chamber of Commerce
Ken Landau
Richard & Olivia Letts
Douglas Lincoln
Daryl Major
Eugenia McCoubrey

Donna Peterson
Caroline S. Pollack
Barb Powers
I.B. Pyka
Zigmond Pyka
James T. Reid
Barbara Ann Robinson
Margaret Schrepfer
Lillian Scieszka
Sohn Linen Service
Jack Stewart
Sparrow Hospital
Robert Stanley
Donald & Kay Staude
Michael Staude
Story Oldsmobile
Bradley L. Throop
Gordie Truman
David Trumpie
Eric Turner
Fred Wappel
Gabrielle Marie Ward

A special thank you to the following
Silver Sponsors

Blue Pencil Creative	The Gregorian
Century Cellunet	Foundation
Emil's Italian Restaurant	Two Men and a Truck
Engineering Graphics	Vision Marketing
Jammin' Design Studio	Walsworth Printing
K.L. Sports	WILS AM FM
Partners Book Distributors	WJIM AM
Spartan Sports Den	WJXQ FM

Greater Lansing Association of Realtors

Sesquicentennial Logo Design by Robert J. Morris

Leavenworth Photographics

Photography for Business and Industry
In Lansing Since 1919

Founded in
Boyne City, Michigan by
R. C. Leavenworth
in 1895

Proud of the past...
Confident of the future

Owner/Photographer • Roger Boettcher, C.P.P.   929 West Street, Lansing, Michigan   Phone 482-4658

Think outside the box.

Imagine if your advertisement was on the air 24 hours a day, 7 days a week to a mass audience without interruption and offered a reach and frequency at a lower cost per thousand than any other advertising media available.

It's not so hard to imagine.

Adams Outdoor Advertising

517-321-2121 • www.adamsoutdoor.com

The Greater Lansing

BUSINESS
MONTHLY

June 1997 Anniversary Issue

June 1997

The Greater Lansing

$2.50

BUSINESS MONTHLY

10th Anniversary

Celebrating 150 Years of a World Class City

LCC Celebrates 40 Years as a Unique Community Resource

Wohlert: Managing Change for 100 Years

Junior Achievement Shows How Business Works

YMCA Celebrates 120 Years of Community Service

*S*erving the Greater Lansing business community for more than 10 years.

Michigan Millers makes Lansing its home for more than 100 years

Michigan Millers Mutual Insurance Company was founded in Lansing in 1881 as one of the first cooperative insurance companies in America by owners of flour milling operations.

The Company has operated its home in the state capital ever since that historic beginning. Its two previous locations still exist today with its present home on East Grand River.

Michigan Millers provides "peace-of-mind" protection for things people value with insurance for their autos, homes, boats, and businesses in its home state of Michigan among others.

For the past 50 years, the Company has marketed its insurance through local independent insurance agents. Michigan Millers has become known as *"the company you can count on."*

120 West Ottawa
1890 - 1929

208 North Capitol
1929 - 1956

Michigan Millers
Mutual Insurance Company

Lansing, Michigan

2425 East Grand River
1956 - Present